outside spine 8/85

outside spine 8/85

CIRCUS

Photographs by AL GIESE

CIRCUS

BEATRICE SCHENK DE REGNIERS

The Viking Press   New York

For circus people

*Grateful acknowledgment is made to Ringling
Brothers & Barnum & Bailey Circus for use of all
photographs, and to Ernie Burch for use of the
photographs of Blinko the Clown.*

Text copyright © 1966 by Beatrice Schenk de Regniers
Photographs copyright © 1966 by Al Giese
All rights reserved
First published in 1966 by The Viking Press, Inc.
625 Madison Avenue, New York, N.Y. 10022
Published simultaneously in Canada by
The Macmillan Company of Canada Limited
Library of Congress catalog card number: AC 66-10432
Pic Bk   1. Circus

SBN 670-22272-0

4   5   6   7   8   78   77   76   75   74

PRINTED IN THE U.S.A.

I went to the circus.
Now any night in bed
I can see a circus...
in my head.

I can smell the circus smell.
I can see the circus sights
and the dizzy razzle-dazzle
of the circus lights....

Oh, the circus men and ladies
Are not like people anywhere.
They never walk like you and me.
They only walk on air.

Swinging swinging swoooooping...oh!
My stomach turns flip-flops here below.

Swooping looping swinging
Stop!
I can't look!
If they fall —
What a drop!

And just when I think
That is all I can stand —
Trrrra BOOM comes the band
and in come the clowns.

The clowns make me feel
So funny-sad-glad
With their sad-funny faces.
I feel good. I feel bad.
I feel mixed-up-happy-sad
when I see the clowns.

Oh, the animals in the circus
Are not like animals anywhere—
It's only in the circus
That you see a bear
riding a motorcycle!

Oh, circus elephants are the danciest.

Circus horses are the prettiest and the pranciest.

Circus lions are the kingliest, howliest.

Circus tigers are the snarliest, prowliest.

The circus people that I see
Are not like me.

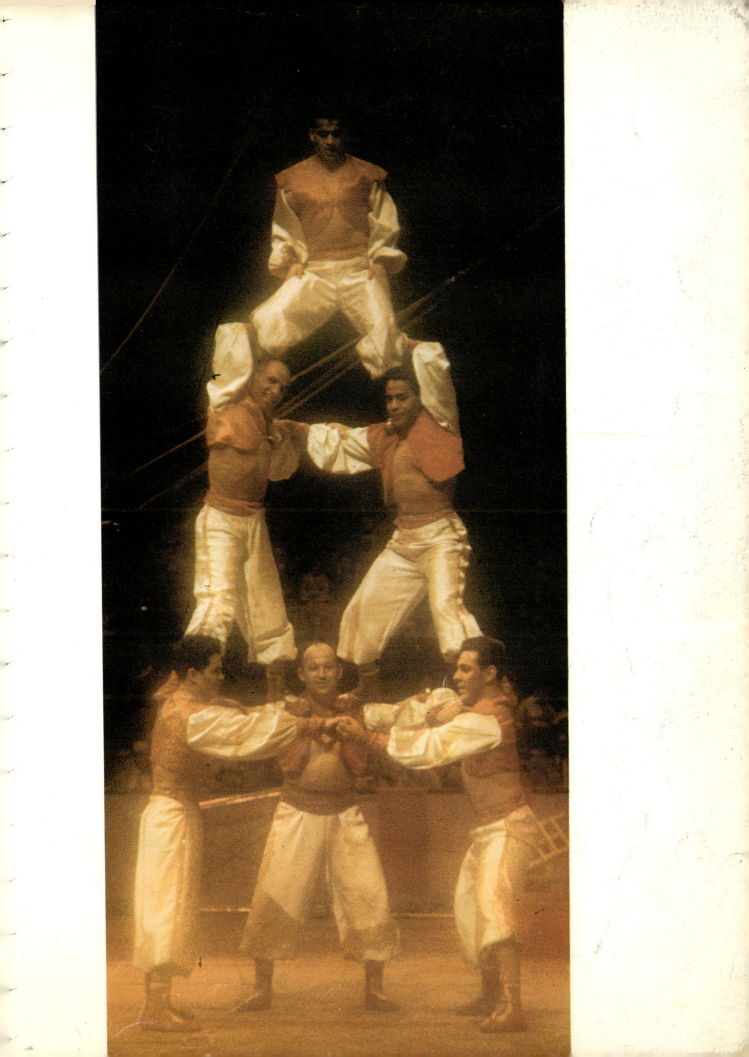

They wear spangles on their clothes
And they dangle by their toes
And there is even one who goes
— and that's the best of all —

Zoom boooooming through a cannon.
She's a human cannon ball.

There is no food in all the world
As fine as circus food.

Clouds of pink spun-sugar fluff
and other stuff.

The crackerjack is crunchier-chewier,
The candy apples stickier-gooier.
The soda pop is fizzlier,
The hot dogs are sizzlier.

Oh, nothing, nothing tastes so good
As razzle-dazzle circus food.

Sound of trumpets.
Sound of drums.

Razzling, dazzling
glitter-clatter.

Now the Big Procession comes.

Is the circus really over?
Oh, never never never!
The circus, the circus
goes on and on forever.
Razzle razzle-dazzle
razzle-dazzle
without
end.